THE JOURNEY OF the one and only

DECLARATION OF INDEPENDENCE

IN CONGR

he unanimous Declaration of

When in the course of human events it become...

...the powers of the earth the separate and equal station to which the Law of Nature...
...the causes which impel them to the separation. _____ We held...
...unalienable Rights, that among these are Life, Liberty and the pursuit of Happiness...
...the consent of the governed. ___ That whenever any form of government becomes...
...laying its foundation on such principles and organizing its powers in such form...
...that Governments long established should not be changed for light and transient causes...
...rather than to right themselves by abolishing the forms to which they are accustomed...
...to reduce them under absolute Despotism, it is their right, it is their duty to throw...
...present year of these colonies; and such is now the necessity which constrains them...
...history of repeated injuries and usurpations...

ESS. JULY 4. 1776.

thirteen united States of America

THE JOURNEY OF the one and only

PUFFIN BOOKS
AN IMPRINT OF PENGUIN GROUP (USA)

DECLARATION OF INDEPENDENCE

JUDITH ST. GEORGE   illustrated by WILL HILLENBRAND

BY 1775, AMERICANS in the thirteen colonies were sick and tired of being ruled by Great Britain and King George. Many of the two and a half million Americans wanted to rule themselves. So they went to war with Great Britain—the Revolutionary War.

Then they wrote the Declaration of Independence. The name says it all. The Declaration of Independence declares that the thirteen American colonies are free and independent states. And all people have equal rights.

What a great document! For more than two hundred years, the Declaration of Independence has been under glass for the world to view and admire. Right?

6

WRONG! THE DECLARATION of Independence has had more homes than a traveling circus. And almost none have been under glass.

Here's how it all began. In 1776, tall, redheaded Thomas Jefferson put his quill pen to paper and the Declaration of Independence sprang to life. On July 4, 1776, members of the Second Continental Congress from the colonies voted to adopt the Declaration—all except New York. But they gave it a ho-hum title: "A Declaration by the Representatives of the United States in General Congress Assembled."

ON JULY 4, 1776, the brand-new document that started up a brand-new country was signed by only two men in Philadelphia's Pennsylvania State House. President of the Congress John Hancock signed it. (He lived in Boston and had lots of money.) Secretary of the Congress Charles Thomson signed it, too. (He didn't have much money, but he was a quick thinker and a good writer.)

Right away, the Declaration was whisked off to John Dunlap's print shop. John Dunlap worked all night printing some twenty-five copies. Charles Thomson pasted one copy in his official journal. Swift-riding couriers delivered the other copies to the thirteen states (no longer colonies).

Farmers, shopkeepers, housewives and people of all ages gathered in every state to hear the Declaration's surprising words. Good-bye to King George III. No more British taxes. No more British soldiers living in their homes. The words were read to General George Washington's troops, too. They had been fighting the Revolutionary War for a year.

Whenever or wherever the surprising words were read, farmers, shopkeepers, housewives and people of all ages shouted YES to the end of British rule. YES to the Declaration of Independence. Huzza! Huzza! Huzza!

ON JULY 9, 1776, New York voted YEA to adopt the Declaration. "The Unanimous Declaration of the Thirteen United States of America" was its fancy new title. Philadelphia's State House bell, later known as the Liberty Bell, pealed all day long. Three huzzas!

To make it official, the Declaration was engrossed—that is, written in large, clear letters on parchment. With a steady hand, quill pen and special ink, Engrosser Timothy Matlack wrote the forty-four lines of the Declaration on a two-foot-wide by two-and-a-half-foot-long sheet of parchment. Every **S** looked like an **F**, but since that was the way people wrote back then, nobody minded.

Signing Day was August 2, 1776. John Hancock signed the engrossed Declaration first. He wrote in big, bold letters so that the British could read his name without spectacles.

Each member of Congress signed by state—Yankee New Englanders (New Hampshire, Massachusetts, Rhode Island, Connecticut); farm-and-seacoast Middle Staters (New York, New Jersey, Pennsylvania, Delaware, Maryland); and slave-holding Southerners (Virginia, North Carolina, South Carolina, Georgia). Five members of Congress signed later—fifty-seven signatures in all. Eager, reluctant, worried or proud, no man wrote his name lightly. The British were sure to call them all TRAITORS.

Once it was signed, the engrossed Declaration became the official, one-and-only Declaration of Independence.

Wow, the official, one-and-only Declaration of Independence was set forever in Philadelphia's handsome brick Pennsylvania State House on Chestnut Street. Right?

WRONG! REVOLUTIONARY WAR cannons were thundering. Bullets were whistling. The new Declaration and the new United States of America were both in danger with a capital *D*.

Members of Congress were in danger, too. So they got nervous in December 1776 when a cry went up: "The British are coming!" Quick-thinking Charles Thomson rolled up the official, one-and-only Declaration of Independence. (Parchment should never be folded.) He loaded it in a light wagon with other important papers. Then, with members of Congress, he made fast tracks for Baltimore, Maryland.

The Declaration—and Congress—snuggled down in the little waterfront town of Baltimore. But three months later, the British still hadn't shown up in Philadelphia. The one-and-only Declaration—and members of Congress—bid farewell to the little waterfront town of Baltimore and trooped back to the Pennsylvania State House.

ON JULY 4, 1777, the Declaration was one year old. So was the United States. Like any one-year-old, the nation was toddling on unsteady feet. The war still hadn't been won. But it hadn't been lost, either.

Philadelphia threw a wingding of a birthday party. The Declaration didn't march in the parade . . . or join the militia in firing a salute . . . or marvel at the sky-high fireworks. But the forty-four-line, one-page parchment was the star of the celebration. Huzza! Huzza! Huzza!

Now the Declaration could be placed under glass in the Pennsylvania State House for all the world to admire. Right?

WRONG! IN SEPTEMBER 1777, the British *did* come—and captured Philadelphia.

But quick-thinking Charles Thomson, the rolled-up Declaration (never folded) and members of Congress had already skipped town. Their home away from home was the courthouse in York, Pennsylvania.

It was a happy day when the British soldiers marched out of Philadelphia nine months later and the one-and-only Declaration returned to the handsome brick Pennsylvania State House. It was an even happier day when the war ended in 1783 (we won).

That was some zigzagging around! If it hadn't been for quick-thinking Charles Thomson, the Declaration might have been stolen. Or misplaced. Or lost in the shuffle. Or even folded.

Just two years later, after traveling to New Jersey (twice) and Maryland (once), the Declaration and members of Congress headed for New York City. Though New York City was mostly farmland, it was the new capital of the United States. Like it or not, for the next five years, New York City Hall's dark and dismal Assembly Room was home to the Declaration—and Congress.

THOSE FIVE YEARS WERE DARK and dismal for the United States, too. Congress governed the country, but the thirteen states were like thirteen spoiled children. They quarreled with one another about their borders, money, taxes and everything else. The United States was definitely NOT united.

Finally, in 1789, a new set of laws called the Constitution of the United States of America became the Law of the Land. George Washington was elected President. Charles Thomson retired. Good job, Charles.

But if Charles was gone, who would watch over the one-and-only Declaration? The new Secretary of State, that's who.

HAPPY DAY! THE SECRETARY of State was the Declaration's author, Thomas Jefferson. And the new capital of the United States was Philadelphia.

Talk about coming home. The Declaration's traveling days were over. Right?

Wrong! The Declaration's traveling days had hardly begun.

In 1800, the government moved lock, stock and barrel to Washington City, the just built, brand-new capital of the United States.

The Declaration boarded a ship in Philadelphia and sailed down the Delaware River out into the Atlantic Ocean. Bucking the waves and with sails billowing, the ship rounded the tip of Virginia, sailed up Chesapeake Bay into the Potomac River and landed in Washington City.

BUT THE ROLLED~UP DECLARATION had nowhere to go in brand-new, just built Washington City. Nowhere. The Declaration trailed after the Secretary of State wherever he had an office. (By 1801, Thomas Jefferson was no longer Secretary of State. He was President.)

No one much cared about the Declaration of Independence anyway. That musty old parchment belonged back in the days of wigs and knee breeches. These were modern times. President Jefferson bought the Louisiana Territory from France in 1803, which almost doubled the size of the United States. Why, more than five million Americans lived in seventeen states. What could the Declaration have to say to such a large and booming country?

But the British were making trouble. The British wanted to control the seas. They were forcing American ships to turn back. They were capturing American sailors to serve on British vessels.

The Declaration wasn't just a musty old parchment after all. The Declaration—and the country—shouted NO to Great Britain. But with that NO, the United States landed plunk in the middle of another war called the War of 1812. (1812 was when the war began.)

Two years later, the United States and Great Britain were still at war. The capital and the Declaration were once again in danger. British forces marched toward Washington. Their goal? Destroy the capital. Quick, slip that rolled-up Declaration in a linen sack, hide the sack in a wagon, hitch up a horse and head for Virginia.

THE BRITISH SET FIRE to most of Washington, even the White House. But the Declaration of Independence was safe and sound thirty-five miles away in a clergyman's Leesburg, Virginia, home. As soon as the British sailed off, the One and Only hightailed it home. Burned-out Washington was quickly rebuilt.

After the War of 1812 (we won), Americans viewed the Declaration with new eyes. Its title called for a UNITED States of America. And the war *had* united America. The country was strong, too, a country that other nations looked up to.

Now proud Americans, whose hands weren't always clean, unrolled, examined, studied, handled, copied and re-rolled the official One and Only. Sometimes people slapped heavy weights on the corners so that the parchment wouldn't curl up. The Declaration began to fade, especially the signatures.

How about making really good copies? Then the official, one-and-only Declaration could retire.

IN 1820, THE SECRETARY of State (the eighth after Thomas Jefferson) hired Engraver William Stone to make copies. Engraver Stone pressed a damp paper on the parchment to imprint the Declaration's words on the paper. (It also lifted off more of the ink.) The damp paper was then pressed on a copper plate, imprinting the Declaration's words on the plate. With a sharp tool, William Stone etched every one of the Declaration's words. The job took him three years.

But the two hundred copies that were run off looked just like the One and Only. Now the Declaration could take it easy. Right?

3 YEARS

Wrong!

In 1841, the Secretary of State (the seventeenth) ordered that the one-and-only Declaration and George Washington's 1775 commission as Commander in Chief of the Army be framed together and hung opposite a window. For thirty-five years, sunlight yellowed the parchment. Hot, humid Washington summers expanded the parchment. Cold, windy Washington winters shrank the parchment.

Those thirty-five years found the country stressed-out, too. The North and South fought a bloody Civil War. More than half a million Americans died. President Abraham Lincoln was assassinated.

By 1876, things were beginning to look up. Money and jobs were tight. BUT a railroad stretched from the Atlantic to the Pacific. Most important, slavery was no more. And the document that promised freedom to every American was one hundred years old—just like the nation.

AS THE HONORED GUEST at Philadelphia's birthday bash, the Declaration of Independence returned to the handsome brick Pennsylvania State House, now called Independence Hall. But home was no longer Charles Thomson's cozy desk. Home was a cold, fireproof safe with glass doors. The Declaration spent nights locked up and days being gawked at.

On July 4, 1876, the Declaration was sprung from lockup. In Philadelphia's Independence Square, the one-hundred-year-old's stirring words were read aloud. The crowds clapped, cheered and shouted loud hurrahs.

One year later, as the country stepped off into its second hundred years, the Declaration stepped off into a new Washington home—the library of the State, War, and Navy Building. But the library had an open fireplace, and smoking—mostly cigars—was allowed. Uh-oh, parchment and smoke were a bad mix.

The Declaration suffered through seventeen years in a smoky haze. Finally, the Secretary of State (the thirty-eighth) had the One and Only carefully wrapped, placed flat between two sheets of glass (not rolled or folded) and locked in a steel case.

THE DECLARATION'S NEXT TWENTY-SIX years were spent under lock and key. By 1920, Americans were fed up. During those twenty-six years, millions of immigrants came to this country to find the freedom that the Declaration offered. And the United States fought (and won) both the Spanish-American War and World War I to become a world power. Americans wanted their Declaration back.

The Secretary of State (the fiftieth) agreed with a thumping YESIREE. The Declaration of Independence should be on display. But where? At the Library of Congress, that's where.

In 1921, the Declaration and the Constitution of the United States chugged across Washington in the Library's Model T Ford mail truck.

NO MORE ROOM!

FULL

TRENCH WARFARE

OVER CROWDED CITIES

WAVES OF IMMIGR

REMEMBER THE MAINE

ROUGH RIDERS VICTORY

A shrine for the Declaration and the Constitution was dedicated in February 1924. No one spoke, not even the President. President Calvin Coolidge was called Silent Cal. No speeches suited him fine. The Declaration and the Constitution were slipped into bronze and glass cases . . . silently. Everyone sang "America," and that was that.

In an open-to-view, guarded-day-and-night shrine where it wouldn't be rolled, copied, smoked on, faded by sunlight or crinkled by cold, the Declaration of Independence found a safe home at last.

Right?

WRONG! THE UNITED STATES ENTERED World War II on December 8, 1941, one day after the Japanese attacked Pearl Harbor. Washington would be a prime bombing target.

Three weeks later, the Declaration and the Constitution raced to the Washington railroad station. They were packed in a bronze container that was padlocked and guarded by Secret Service agents. Hustled aboard a train, they sped to their secret destination—Fort Knox, Kentucky. Their new home? Gold Bullion Compartment Number 24.

RIGHT AWAY THE DECLARATION had a physical. At 165 years old, the Declaration almost flunked. The parchment was dotted with glue spots and tiny holes. A glob of glue and Scotch tape held the torn right corner together. Cracks crisscrossed the forty-four lines of writing. Some long-ago person had folded the document. Bring in the repair experts. Two days later, the Declaration was in tip-top shape.

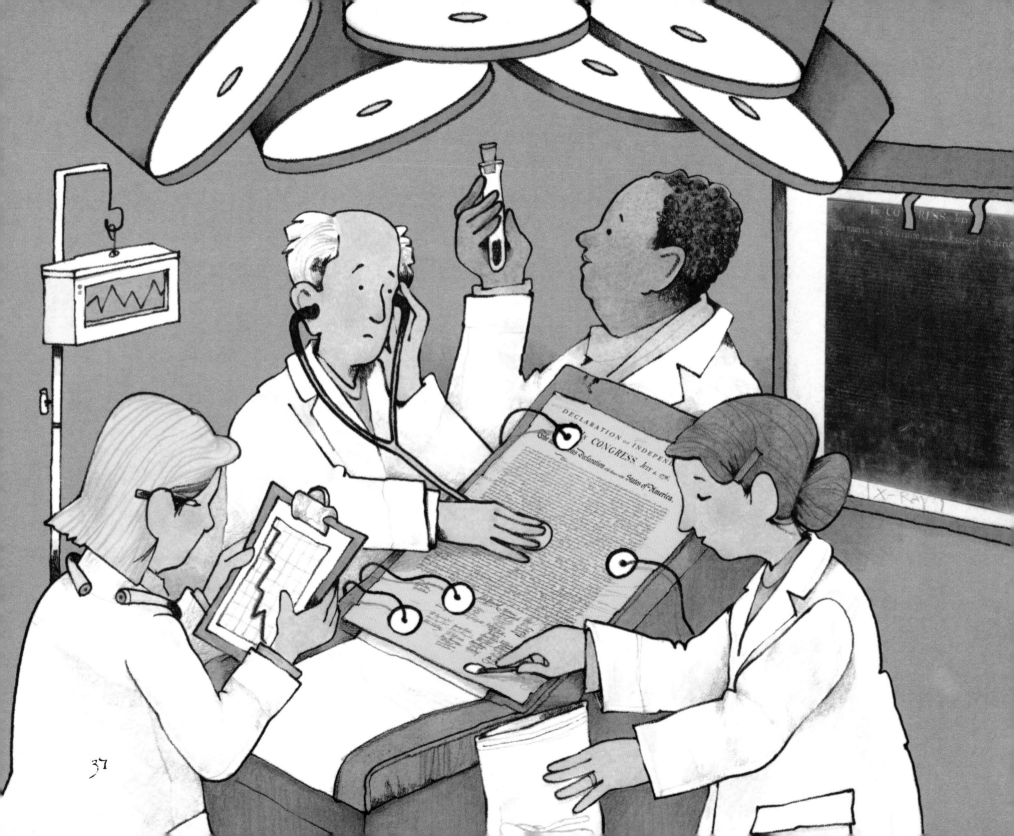

FORT KNOX WAS A STRANGE PLACE to call home. But during World War II, every American's life was strange. Husbands, fathers, sons and brothers fought and died all over the world. Wives, mothers, daughters and sisters joined the military and worked for the war effort at men's jobs.

War news turned upbeat in 1944. The Declaration of Independence and the Constitution headed home to Washington. After the war (we won), millions of servicemen and women happily headed home, too.

The Declaration of Independence resided at the Library of Congress from then on. Right?

A-BOMB

WRONG! THE GOVERNMENT HAD other plans up its sleeve.

The impressive stone National Archives Building on Pennsylvania Avenue was built in the 1930s to hold historic documents. And Mr. National Archivist had his eye on America's most historic document—the Declaration of Independence.

But the Declaration was Mr. Librarian of Congress's number-one treasure. Visitors from all over the world came to the Library to see the sheet of parchment that held out hope to all people.

Mr. Librarian and Mr. Archivist argued politely for years. The Declaration had been engrossed, signed, printed, copied, engraved and repaired, but it had never been fought over, politely or not. The winner? Mr. Archivist.

Moving Day was December 13, 1952. Twelve Armed Forces Special Police carried the Declaration and the Constitution in wooden crates down the Library's steps through two rows of servicewomen. They boarded their chariot, a Marine Corps tank. Was a sad Mr. Librarian of Congress watching from an upstairs window?

Escorted by a color guard, Army Band, Air Force Drum and Bugle Corps, two light tanks, servicemen carrying submachine guns AND four motorcycles, the tank rumbled its way to the National Archives Building. President Harry Truman and lots of VIPs (Very Important People) welcomed the Declaration and the Constitution to their new home. As they should have. After all, the two documents had held the country on a steady course through eight wars, two attacks on the nation's capital, a four-year split between North and South, and three Presidents assassinated.

The Archivist and Librarian of Congress, still polite, pulled back ceiling-high curtains. There they were, the Constitution of the United States, the Bill of Rights, and high above the others in the place of honor? The Declaration of Independence.

THE ONE AND ONLY, two by two-and-a-half foot parchment had earned that place of honor. It had traveled by horseback, carriage, wagon, sailing vessel, handcart, mail truck, railroad car, armed truck and Marine Corps tank. It had been stuffed in courier pouches, closets, cabinets, desk drawers, linen sacks and steel cases.

No effort was too much to keep the Declaration of Independence safe. It declares the birth of a new nation. It celebrates the value and dignity of every human being. Though it doesn't declare that all people are created equal in ability, talent or brains, it does declare that all people are created equal in their basic rights, including "life, liberty, and the pursuit of happiness."

43

Now, protected by armed guards, a twenty-four-hour-a-day camera and an electronic monitor, the engrossed, signed Declaration of Independence had at last found its true and forever home.

Right?

BOTH RIGHT AND WRONG! In practical terms, the Declaration of Independence had found its true and forever home in the impressive stone National Archives Building.

But in terms of the human spirit, the Declaration has had a true and forever home right from the start. Old, torn, faded, admired, neglected, loved or criticized, the Declaration's home has always been in the heart of the American people.

DECLARATION of INDEPENDENCE

IN CONGRESS, July 4, 1776.

The unanimous Declaration of the thirteen united States of America.

45

BIBLIOGRAPHY

Carlin, John W. "A Birthday Party You Won't Want to Miss." *Prologue: Quarterly of the National Archives and Records Administration* 33 (Summer 2001): 72–73, 122–127.

Goff, Frederick R. *The John Dunlap Broadside: The First Printing of the Declaration of Independence.* Washington, D.C.: Library of Congress, 1976.

Gustafson, Milton O. "The Empty Shrine: The Transfer of the Declaration of Independence and the Constitution to the National Archives." *American Archivist* 39 (July 1976): 271–285.

Hazelton, John H. *The Declaration of Independence: Its History*. New York: Dodd, Mead and Company, 1906.

Lucas, Stephen E. "The Stylistic Artistry of the Declaration of Independence." *Prologue*: *Quarterly of the National Archives and Records Administration* 22 (Spring 1990): 25–43.

Malone, Dumas. *The Story of the Declaration of Independence*. New York: Oxford University Press, 1954.

Mearns, David C. *The Declaration of Independence: The Story of a Parchment.* Washington, D.C.: United States Printing Office, 1950.

National Archives Trust Fund Board. "Declaration of Independence: The Adventures of a Document." National Archives and Records Service: 5–42. Washington, D.C.: General Services Administration, 1976.

Acknowledgments:
Many, many thanks to Rob (my Congressman) and Jane Portman and his family—Jed, Will and Sally.
In addition, thanks to Linda Elliott Long, Roxanne Maier, and Mr. Harrington at the USPS in D.C.,
who were all a part of the journey of this book.   —W.H.

Love to Sarah and her family. —J.St.G.

To Trina, who believed in me.
With special thanks to Patti and Semadar, for their confidence,
patience and friendship. —W.H.

PATRICIA LEE GAUCH, EDITOR

PUFFIN BOOKS
Published by the Penguin Group
Penguin Group (USA) LLC
375 Hudson Street
New York, New York 10014

USA * Canada * UK * Ireland * Australia
New Zealand * India * South Africa * China

penguin.com
A Penguin Random House Company

First published in the United States of America by Philomel Books, a division of Penguin Young Readers Group, 2005
Published by Puffin Books, an imprint of Penguin Young Readers Group, 2014

Text copyright © 2005 by Judith St. George
Illustrations copyright © 2005 by Will Hillenbrand

THE LIBRARY OF CONGRESS HAS CATALOGED THE PHILOMEL BOOKS EDITION AS FOLLOWS:
St. George, Judith, date.   The journey of the one and only Declaration of Independence / Judith St. George ;
illustrated by Will Hillenbrand.   p. cm.   Includes bibliographical references.
ISBN 0-399-23738-0 (hardcover)
1. United States. Declaration of Independence—Juvenile literature. 2. United States—Politics and government—1775–1783—Juvenile literature.
I. Hillenbrand, Will. II. Title.   E221.S725 2005   973.3'13—dc22   2004013567

Puffin Books ISBN 978-0-14-751164-5

Manufactured in China

1 3 5 7 9 10 8 6 4 2